The Sexual Offences Act 2003

Fergus Smith
B.Sc(Hons), M.A., C.Q.S.W.,D.M.S., Dip.M

in consultation with

Paul Carr
M.A.(Cantab)
District Judge (Magistrates'Courts)

Children Act Enterprises Ltd (CAE)
103 Mayfield Road
South Croydon
Surrey CR2 0BH

www.caeuk.org

© Fergus Smith

British Library Cataloguing in Publication Data
A catalogue record for this book is available from the
British Library

ISBN 1 899986 86 3

Designed and typeset by Andrew Haig & Associates
Printed in the UK by The Lavenham Press

CAE is an independent organisation which publishes
guides to family and criminal law and provides
consultancy, research, training and independent
investigation services to the public, private and voluntary
sectors.

Contents

ACA 2002 = Adoption and Children Act 2002
CA 1989 = Children Act 1989
DVCVB = Domestic Violence, Crime and Victims Bill 2003

References in square brackets are to sections and schedules of the Sexual Offences Act 2003 unless otherwise stated.

Italicised words within text are defined in ss.78 and 79 of SOA 2003 and summarised in the definitions section of this guide.

Unless the offence can apply only to a male or a female, this guide uses the term 's/he' throughout.

Introduction

- This guide is designed for use by all those in England and Wales whose work is in any way concerned with the education, care or protection of children e.g. teachers, social workers, police officers, probation officers and health professionals.

- It aims to provide easy access to and reinforce understanding of those provisions relevant to children and young people, of an Act described as the most radical overhaul of sex offences legislation for over 50 years.

- The Sexual Offences Bill was published in January 2003 and its provisions were based upon:
  - The White Paper published in November 2002 and entitled 'Protecting the Public: Strengthening Protection Against Sex Offenders and Reforming the Law on Sexual Offences (Cm 5668).'
  - An earlier independent review, the recommendations of which had been set out for public consultation in a paper published in 2000 entitled 'Setting the Boundaries' and
  - A government review of the Sex Offenders Act 1997

- This guide should be used to supplement or reinforce, not replace reference to legislation itself, associated regulations or official guidance.

  NB. The Sexual Offences Act 2003 was implemented in full on May 1 2004.

Key Points

- The Act strengthens protection for children e.g. any sexual intercourse with a child aged less than 13 will be charged as rape.

- A range of new offences are introduced and designed to tackle all inappropriate activity with children.

- A civil order to apply to internet and off-line grooming will enable restrictions to be placed on people displaying inappropriate behaviour before an offence is committed.

- Maximum penalties for sexual offences against children have been raised to reflect the severity of the crimes.

- The Act updates offences relating to sexual activity with a family member to better reflect the modern family.

- Penalties with respect to offences relating to sexual violence and exploitation are strengthened.

- The Act introduces measures to achieve equality with respect to men and women.

- The role of those providing advice to children on sexual issues is recognised and exemptions introduced from prosecution for aiding and abetting a child's offence.

Definitions

Consent [s.74]

■ For the purposes of Part 1 of the Act (in practice
ss.1–4 only), a person *consents* if s/he agrees by
choice and has the freedom and capacity to make
that choice.

*NB. See also further relevant provisions under s.1 and
ss. 2–4 described below.*

General Interpretation for Purpose of Part 1 [s.79]

■ *Penetration* is a continuing act from entry to
withdrawal [s.79(2)]

■ References to a *part of the body* include references
to a part surgically constructed (in particular through
gender reassignment surgery) [s.79)(3)]

■ *Image* means a moving or still image and includes
an image produced by any means and, where the
context permits, a three dimensional image [s.79(4)]

■ References to an *image of a person* include references
to an image of an imaginary person [s.79(5)]

■ *Mental disorder* has the meaning given it by s.1
Mental Health Act 1983 [s.79(6)] i.e. mental illness,
arrested or incomplete development of mind,
psychopathic disorder and any other disorder or
disability of mind.

- References to *observation* (however expressed) are to observation whether direct or by looking at an image [s.79(7)]

- *Touching* includes touching with any part of the body; with anything else; through anything and in particular, includes touching amounting to penetration [s.79(8)]

- *Vagina* includes vulva [s.79(9)]

- *In relation to an animal*, references to vagina or anus include references to any similar part [s.79(10)]

Sexual [s.78]

- For the purposes of Part 1 of the Act (except s.71 – sexual activity in a public lavatory), penetration, touching or any other activity is *sexual* if a reasonable person would consider that:
  - Whatever its circumstances or any person's purpose in relation to it, it is because of its nature sexual or
  - Because of its nature it may be sexual and because of its circumstances or the purpose of any person in relation to it (or both) it is sexual

Part 1: Sexual Offences

Rape

Rape [s.1]

- A person (A) commits an offence of rape if:
  - He intentionally *penetrates* the *vagina*, anus or mouth of another person (B) with his penis
  - B does not *consent* to the penetration and
  - A does not reasonably believe that B consents

  NB. Whether a belief is reasonable is to be determined having regard to all the circumstances, including any steps A has taken to ascertain whether B consents.

  A person guilty of an offence under s.1 is liable, on conviction on indictment (i.e. a case triable in the case of an adult only at the Crown Court), to life imprisonment.

- **Evidential presumptions about consent**: The complainant is to be taken not to have consented to the relevant act unless sufficient evidence is adduced to raise an issue as to her/his consent, and the defendant is to be taken not to have reasonably believed that the complainant consented unless sufficient evidence is adduced to raise this possibility **if** in proceedings for an offence under this section:
  - It is proved the defendant did the relevant act
  - That any of the circumstances described below existed and
  - The defendant knew that those circumstances existed

- The circumstances are that:
  - Any person was at the time of the relevant act or immediately before it began, using violence against the complainant or causing the complainant to fear that immediate violence would be used against her/him
  - Any person was at the time of the relevant act or immediately before it began, causing the complainant to fear that violence was being used or that immediate violence would be used against another person
  - The complainant was, and the defendant was not, unlawfully detained at the time of the relevant act
  - The complainant was asleep or otherwise unconscious at the time of the relevant act
  - Because of the complainant's physical disability, the complainant would not have been able to at the time of the relevant act to communicate to the defendant whether the complaint consented
  - Any person had administered to or caused to be taken by the complainant without her/his consent, a substance which, having regard to when administered or taken, was capable of causing or enabling the complainant to be stupefied or overpowered at the time of the relevant act [s.75]

NB. The reference in the first 2 bullet points above to the time immediately before the relevant act began is, in the case of an act which is one of a continuous series of sexual activities, a reference to the time immediately before the first one.

- **Conclusive presumptions about consent**: If in proceedings for an offence to which s.76 applies it is proved that the defendant did the relevant act and that any of the circumstance specified below applied, it is to be conclusively presumed that:
  - The complainant did not consent to the relevant act
  - The defendant did not believe that s/he consented

- Those circumstances are that:
  - The defendant intentionally deceived the complainant as to the nature or purpose of the relevant act
  - The defendant intentionally induced the complainant to consent to the relevant act by impersonating a person know personally to the complainant

Assault

Assault by Penetration [s.2]

■ A person (A) commits an offence if:
  - S/he intentionally *penetrates* the *vagina or* anus of another person (B) with a part of her/his body or anything else
  - The penetration is '*sexual*'
  - B does not *consent* to the penetration and
  - A does not 'reasonably' believe that B consents

  NB. Whether a belief is reasonable is to be determined having regard to all the circumstances, including any steps A has taken to ascertain whether B consents [s.2(2)].

■ A person guilty of an offence under s.2 is liable, on conviction on indictment to life imprisonment [s.2(4)].

  NB. See also material on 'evidential' and 'conclusive' presumptions about consent (which are also applicable to ss.2–4) under s.1 above.

Sexual Assault [s.3]

■ A person (A) commits an offence of sexual assault if:
  - S/he intentionally *touches* another person (B)
  - The touching is *sexual*
  - B does not *consent* to the touching and
  - A does not reasonably believe that B consents

NB. Whether a belief is reasonable is to be determined having regard to all the circumstances, including any steps A has taken to ascertain whether B consents.

A person guilty of an offence under s.3 is liable on summary conviction to imprisonment for a term not exceeding 6 months or a fine not exceeding the statutory limit or both and on conviction on indictment, to imprisonment for a term not exceeding 10 years.

See also material on 'evidential' and 'conclusive' presumptions about consent (which are also applicable to ss.2–4) under s.1 above.

Causing Sexual Activity without Consent

Causing a Person to Engage in Sexual Activity without Consent [s.4]

- A person (A) commits an offence of causing a person to engage in sexual activity without consent if:
    - S/he intentionally causes another person (B) to engage in an activity
    - The activity is *sexual*
    - B does not *consent* to engaging in the activity and
    - A does not reasonably believe that B consents

    NB. Whether a belief is reasonable is to be determined having regard to all the circumstances, including any steps A has taken to ascertain whether B consents [s.4 (2).

- s.4(4) states that a person guilty of an offence under s.4, is liable, on conviction on indictment, to imprisonment for life if the activity caused involved penetration of:
    - B's anus or *vagina*
    - B's mouth or with a person's penis
    - A person's anus or vagina with a part of B's body or by B with anyone else or
    - Of a person's mouth with B's penis

■ If the offence did not involve penetration as above, the offender is liable:

- On summary conviction to a maximum 6 months imprisonment, a fine not exceeding the statutory limit or both

- On conviction on indictment (i.e. triable in the case of an adult only in the Crown Court), to imprisonment for a term not exceeding 10 years [s.4(5)]

NB. See also material on 'evidential' and 'conclusive' presumptions about consent (which are also applicable to ss.2–4) under s.1 above.

Rape & Other Offences Against Children under 13

Rape of a Child under 13 [s.5]

- ■ A person commits an offence of rape of a child under 13 if he:
  - • Intentionally penetrates the *vagina*, anus or mouth of another person with his penis and
  - • The other person is aged less than 13 years old

- ■ A person guilty of an offence under s.5 is liable, on conviction on indictment (i.e. triable in the case of an adult only at the Crown Court), to imprisonment for life.

Assault by Penetration of a Child under 13 [s.6]

- ■ A person commits an offence of assault by penetration of a child if:
  - • S/he intentionally penetrates the *vagina* or anus of another person with a *part of her/his body* or anything else
  - • The penetration is *sexual* and
  - • The other person is under 13

- ■ A person guilty of an offence under s.6 is liable, on conviction on indictment, to imprisonment for life.

Sexual Assault of a Child under 13 [s.7]

- A person commits an offence of sexual assault if:
  - S/he intentionally *touches* another person
  - The touching is *sexual* and
  - The other person is under 13

- A person guilty of an offence under s.7 is liable:
  - On summary conviction, to a maximum of 6 months imprisonment, a fine not exceeding the statutory maximum or both
  - On conviction on indictment (i.e. triable in the case of an adult only in the Crown Court), to imprisonment for a maximum of 14 years

Causing or Inciting a Child under 13 to Engage in Sexual Activity [s.8]

- A person commits an offence of causing or inciting a child under 13 to engage in sexual activity if:
  - S/he intentionally causes or incites another person (B) to engage in an activity
  - The activity is *sexual* and
  - B is under 13

- A person found guilty on conviction on indictment (i.e. triable in the case of an adult only in the Crown Court), under s.8 may be imprisoned for life if the activity caused or incited, involved:
  - Penetration of B's anus or *vagina*
  - Penetration of B's mouth with a person's penis

- Penetration of a person's anus or vagina with a part of B's body or by B with anything else or
- Penetration of a person's mouth with B's penis

■ Unless the conditions above applied, a person guilty of a s.8 offence is liable:
  - On summary conviction, to imprisonment for a maximum of 6 months, a fine not exceeding the maximum amount or both
  - On conviction on indictment (i.e. triable in the case of an adult only in the Crown Court), to a maximum of 14 years imprisonment

Child Sex Offences

Sexual Activity with a Child [s.9]

■ A person aged 18 or over (A) commits an offence of sexual activity with a child if:
- S/he intentionally *touches* another person (B)
- The touching is *sexual* and
- Either B is under 16 and A does not reasonably believe that B is 16 or over **or** B is under 13 [s.9(1)]

■ A person guilty of a s.9 offence is liable, on conviction on indictment to a maximum 14 years imprisonment if the touching involved:
- *Penetration* of B's mouth with A's penis
- Penetration of A's anus or vagina with a part of B's body or
- Penetration of a A's mouth with B's penis [s.9(2)]

■ Unless the conditions above applied, a person guilty of a s.9 offence is liable:
- On summary conviction, to imprisonment for a maximum of 6 months, a fine not exceeding the maximum amount or both
- On conviction on indictment (i.e. triable in the case of an adult only in the Crown Court) , to a maximum of 14 years imprisonment [s.9(3)]

Causing or Inciting a Child to Engage in Sexual Activity [s.10]

■ A person aged 18 or over (A) commits an offence of causing or inciting a child to engage in sexual activity if:
  • S/he intentionally causes or incites another person (B) to engage in an activity
  • The activity is *sexual* and
  • Either B is under 16 and A does not reasonably believe that B is 16 or over **or** B is under 13 [s.10(1)]

■ A person guilty of a s.10 offence is liable, on conviction on indictment (i.e. triable in the case of an adult only in the Crown Court) to a maximum 14 years imprisonment if the activity cause or incited involved:
  • *Penetration* of B's anus or vagina
  • Penetration of B's mouth with a person's penis
  • Penetration of a persons' anus or vagina with a *part of B's body* or by B with anything else or
  • Penetration of a person's mouth with B's penis [s.10(2)]

■ Unless the conditions above applied, a person guilty of a s.10 offence is liable:
  • On summary conviction, to imprisonment for a maximum of 6 months, a fine not exceeding the maximum amount or both
  • On conviction on indictment (i.e. triable in the case of an adult only in the Crown Court), to a maximum of 14 years imprisonment [s.10(3)]

Engaging in Sexual Activity in the Presence of a Child [s.11]

- A person aged 18 or over (A) commits an offence of engaging in sexual activity in the presence of a child if:
  - S/he intentionally engages in an activity
  - The activity is *sexual*
  - For the purposes of obtaining sexual gratification, s/he engages in it when another person (B) is present or is in a place from which A can be observed and, knowing or believing B is aware, or intending B should be aware that s/he is engaging in it
  - Either B is under 16 and A does not reasonably believe that B is 16 or over **or** B is under 13 [s.11(1)]

- A person guilty of a s.11 offence is liable:
  - On summary conviction, to imprisonment for a maximum of 6 months, a fine not exceeding the maximum amount or both
  - On conviction on indictment (i.e. triable in the case of an adult only in the Crown Court), to a maximum of 10 years imprisonment [s.11(2)]

Causing a Child to Watch a Sexual Act [s.12]

- A person aged 18 or over (A) commits an offence of causing a child to watch a sexual act if:
  - For the purposes of obtaining sexual gratification, s/he intentionally causes another person (B) to watch a third person engaging in

an activity, or to look at an image of any person engaging in an activity
- The activity is *sexual* and
- Either B is under 16 and A does not reasonably believe that B is 16 or over **or** B is under 13 [s.12(1)]

- A person guilty of a s.12 offence is liable:
  - On summary conviction, to imprisonment for a maximum of 6 months, a fine not exceeding the maximum amount or both
  - On conviction on indictment (i.e. triable in the case of an adult only in the Crown Court), to a maximum of 10 years imprisonment [s.12(2)]

Child Sex Offences Committed by Children or Young Persons [s.13]

- A person under 18 commits an offence if s/he does anything which would be an offence under any of sections 9–12 if s/he were aged 18 [s.13(1)].

- A person guilty of a s.13 offence is liable:
  - On summary conviction, to imprisonment for a maximum of 6 months, a fine not exceeding the maximum amount or both
  - On conviction on indictment (i.e. triable in the case of an adult only in the Crown Court), to a maximum of 5 years imprisonment [s.13(2)]

Arranging or Facilitating Commission of a Child Sex Offence [s.14]

■ A person commits an offence of arranging or facilitating commission of a child sex offence if:
- S/he intentionally arranges or facilitates something that s/he intends to do, intends another person to do, or believes that another person will do, in any part of the world, and
- Doing it will involve the commission of an offence under any of the sections 9–13 [s.14(1)]

■ A person does not commit an offence under s.14 if:
- S/he arranges or facilitates something s/he believes another person will do, but that s/he does not intend to do or intend another person to do and
- Any offence as in s.14(1) above would be an offence against a child for whose protection s/he acts

■ For the above purpose, 'protection of a child' by definition excludes acting for the purpose of obtaining sexual gratification or for the purpose of causing or encouraging the offence under s.14(1)(b) or the child's participation in it, and means:
- Protecting the child from sexually transmitted infections
- Protecting the physical safety of a child
- Preventing the child from becoming pregnant or
- Promoting the child's emotional well-being by giving advice [s.14(3)]

NB. This provision offers protection to relevant professionals such as doctors, counsellors etc who are acting in the best interests of sexually active young people.

- A person guilty of a s.14 offence is liable:
  - On summary conviction, to imprisonment for a maximum of 6 months, a fine not exceeding the maximum amount or both
  - On conviction on indictment (i.e. triable in the case of an adult only in the Crown Court), to a maximum of 14 years imprisonment [s.14(4)]

Meeting a Child Following Sexual Grooming etc [s.15]

- A person aged 18 or over (A) commits an offence of meeting a child following sexual grooming if:
  - Having met or communicated with another person (B) on at least 2 earlier occasions, s/he intentionally meets B or travels with the intention of meeting B in any part of the world
  - At the time, s/he intends to do anything to or in respect of B, during or after the meeting and in any part of the world, which if done will involve the commission by A of a 'relevant offence'
  - B is under 16
  - Person A does not reasonably believe that B is 16 or over [s.15(1)]

NB. The reference to A having met or communicated with B means in, from and to and by any means from any part of the world[s.15(2)].

Relevant offence means an offence under Part of the Act, within any of paragraphs 61–92 of Sch.3 or anything done outside of England, Wales and Northern Ireland which would be a Part 1 offence if committed in those jurisdictions [s.15(2)(b)].

- A person guilty of an offence under s.15 is liable:
  - On summary conviction, to imprisonment for a maximum of 6 months, a fine not exceeding the maximum amount or both
  - On conviction on indictment (i.e. triable in the case of an adult only in the Crown Court), to a maximum of 10 years imprisonment [s.15(4)]

Abuse of Position of Trust

Positions of Trust [s.21]

■ For the purposes of defining an offence which is an 'abuse of position oftrust' (ss.16 to 19), a person (A) is in a position of trust in relation to another person (B) if A:

- Looks after persons aged under 18 who are detained in an institution by virtue of a court order or enactment and B is detained there [s.21(2)]
- Looks after under 18 year olds resident in a local authority or voluntary organisation's children's home as defined by the Children Act 1989 and B is provided with accommodation and maintenance there [s.21(3)]
- Looks after under 18 year olds in a hospital, independent clinic, care or residential care home, private hospital, community or voluntary or children's home, home provided under s.82(5) Children Act 1989 or residential family centre and B is accommodated and care for there [s.21(4)]
- Looks after under 18 year olds receiving education at an educational institution and B is receiving education and A is not [s.21(5)]
- Is engaged in provision of services under ss.8–10 Employment and Training Act 1973 or s.114 Learning and Skills Act 2000 and in that capacity, looks after B on an individual basis [s.21(6)]

- Regularly has unsupervised contact with B (face to face or by other means) in the exercise of functions under ss.20 and 21 Children Act 1989 [s.21(8)]
- Reporting to the court in the exercise of s.7 Children Act 1989 duties relating to the welfare of B, regularly has unsupervised contact (face to face or by any other means) [s.21(9)]
- Is a personal adviser for B appointed under s.23B(2) or paragraph 19C Sch. 2 Children Act 1989 [s.21(10)] and in that capacity looks after B on an individual basis
- Looks after B on an individual basis in pursuance of a Care, Supervision or an Education Supervision Order to which B is subject [s.21(11)]
- Is an officer appointed under s.41 Children Act 1989 or a children's guardian under Adoption Act rules who regularly has unsupervised contact (face to face or by any other means) with B [s.21(12)]
- Looks after B on an individual basis in fulfilling duties arising from B being subject to requirements by or under an enactment on her/his release from detention for a criminal offence or because B is subject to court requirements made in criminal proceedings

- Interpretations of a 'position of trust' are offered in s.22 with respect to the terms:
  - Looks after person under 18
  - Individual basis

- Receiving education
- Authority
- Care and residential care home
- Care Order
- Children's, community and voluntary home
- Residential family centre
- Supervision Order and Education Supervision Order
- Hospital and private hospital
- Independent clinic

Abuse of Position of Trust: Sexual Activity with a Child [s.16]

■ A person aged 18 or over (A) commits an offence if:
  - S/he intentionally *touches* another person (B)
  - The touching is *sexual*
  - Person A is in a position of trust (see above for definition) in relation to B
  - Where 'conditions' described below apply, A knows or could reasonably be expected to know of the circumstances by virtue of which s/he is in a position of trust in relation to B and
  - Either B is under 18 and A does not reasonably believe that B is 18 or over or B is under 13 [s.16(1)]

■ The conditions are that A is in a position of trust in relation to B by virtue of the circumstances of s.21(2), (3), (4) or (5) and no others [s.16(2)].

  NB. Where it is proved that B was under 18, it will be assumed the defendant knew this, unless sufficient evidence is adduced to raise an issue as to whether s/he reasonably believed B was 18 or over [s.16(3)]. It will also be assumed the defendant knew s/he was in a position of trust unless sufficient evidence is adduced to overturn this assumption [s.16 (4)].

■ A person found guilty of a s.16 offence is liable:
  • On summary conviction to imprisonment for up to 6 months, a fine not exceeding the statutory limit or both
  • On conviction on indictment (i.e. triable in the case of an adult only in the Crown Court), to imprisonment for up to 5 years [s.16(5)]

Abuse of Position of Trust: Causing or Inciting a Child to Engage in Sexual Activity [s.17]

■ A person aged 18 or over (A) commits an offence if:
  • S/he causes or incites another person (B) to engage in an activity
  • The activity is *sexual*
  • Person A is in a position of trust in relation to B
  • Where 'conditions' described below apply, A knows or could reasonably be expected to know of the circumstances by virtue of which s/he is in a position of trust in relation to B and
  • Either B is under 18 and A does not reasonably believe that B is 18 or over or B is under 13 [s.17(1)]

■ The conditions are that A is in a position of trust in relation to B by virtue of the circumstances of s.21(2), (3), (4) or (5) and no others [s.17(2)]

NB. Where it is proved that B was under 18, it will be assumed the defendant knew this, unless sufficient evidence is adduced to raise an issue as to whether s/he reasonably believed B was 18 or over [s.17(3)]. It will also be assumed the defendant knew s/he was in a position of trust unless sufficient evidence is adduced to overturn this assumption [s.17 (4)].

- ▩ A person found guilty of a s.17 offence is liable:
    - • On summary conviction to imprisonment for up to 6 months, a fine not exceeding the statutory limit or both
    - • On conviction on indictment (i.e. triable in the case of an adult only in the Crown Court), to imprisonment for up to 5 years [s.17(5)]

Abuse of Position of Trust: Sexual Activity in the Presence of a Child [s.18]

- ▩ A person aged 18 or over (A) commits an offence if:
    - • S/he intentionally engages in an activity
    - • The activity is *sexual*
    - • For the purposes of obtaining sexual gratification, s/he engages in it when another person (B) is present or is in a place from which person A can be *observed* and when s/he knows or believes that B is aware, or intends that B should be aware that s/he is engaging in it
    - • Person A is in a *position of trust* in relation to B and
    - • Where 'conditions' described below apply, A knows or could reasonably be expected to know

of the circumstances by virtue of which s/he is in a position of trust in relation to B and

- Either B is under 18 and A does not reasonably believe that B is 18 or over or B is under 13 [s.18(1)]

■ The conditions are that A is in a position of trust in relation to B by virtue of the circumstances of s.21(2), (3), (4) or (5) and no others [s.18(2)]

NB. Where it is proved that B was under 18, it will be assumed the defendant knew this, unless sufficient evidence is adduced to raise an issue as to whether s/he reasonably believed B was 18 or over [s.18(3)]. It will also be assumed the defendant knew s/he was in a position of trust unless sufficient evidence is adduced to overturn this assumption [s.18 (4)].

■ A person found guilty of a s.18 offence is liable:
- On summary conviction to imprisonment for up to 6 months, a fine not exceeding the statutory limit or both
- On conviction on indictment (i.e. triable in the case of an adult only in the Crown Court), to imprisonment for up to 5 years [s.18(5)]

Abuse of Position of Trust: Causing a Child to Watch a Sexual Act [s.19]

■ A person aged 18 or over (A) commits an offence if:
- For the purposes of obtaining sexual gratification, s/he intentionally causes another person (B) to watch a third person engaging in

an activity, or to look at an *image* of any person engaging in an activity
- The activity is *sexual*
- Person A is in a position of trust in relation to B and
- Where 'conditions' described below apply, A knows or could reasonably be expected to know of the circumstances by virtue of which s/he is in a position of trust in relation to B and
- Either B is under 18 and A does not reasonably believe that B is 18 or over or B is under 13 [s.19(1)]

■ The conditions are that A is in a position of trust in relation to B by virtue of the circumstances of s.21(2), (3), (4) or (5) and no others [s.19(2)]

NB. Where it is proved that B was under 18, it will be assumed the defendant knew this, unless sufficient evidence is adduced to raise an issue as to whether s/he reasonably believed B was 18 or over [s.19(3)]. It will also be assumed the defendant knew s/he was in a position of trust unless sufficient evidence is adduced to overturn this assumption [s.19 (4)].

■ A person found guilty of a s.19 offence is liable:
- On summary conviction to imprisonment for up to 6 months, a fine not exceeding the statutory limit or both
- On conviction on indictment (i.e. triable in the case of an adult only in the Crown Court), to imprisonment for up to 5 years [s.19(5)]

NB. Anything which if done in England and Wales or Northern Ireland, would constitute an offence under any of sections 16–19 also constitutes that offence if done in Scotland [s.20].

Marriage Exception [s.23]

■ Conduct by a person (A) which would otherwise be an offence against person (B) under ss. 16–19 is not an offence if B is 16 or over and A and B are lawfully married [s.23].

NB. The defendant must prove that A and B were lawfully married at the time of any given conduct.

Sexual Relationships which Pre-Date Position of Trust [s.24]

■ Unless that relationship is itself unlawful, conduct by a person (A) which would otherwise be an offence against another person (B) under any of ss.16 -19 is not an offence if, immediately before the position of trust arose, a sexual relationship existed between A and B [s.24(1) & (2)]

NB. In ss. 16–19 proceedings, it is for the defendant to prove that such a relationship existed at that time [s.24(3)]

Familial Child Sex Offences

Sexual Activity with a Family Member [s.25]

- A person (A) commits an offence if:
  - S/he intentionally *touches* another person (B)
  - The touching is *sexual*
  - The relation of A to B falls within those relationships defined in s.27 as a 'family relationship' (see below)
  - Person A knows or could reasonably be expected to know that her/his relation to B does fall with one defined in s.27 and
  - Either B is under 18 and A does not reasonably believe that B is 18 or over, or B is under 13

  NB. Where it is proved that B was under 18, it will be assumed the defendant knew this, unless sufficient evidence is adduced to raise an issue as to whether s/he reasonably believed B was 18 or over [s.25(2)]. It will also be assumed the defendant knew that her/his relation to B fell within one of those defined by s.27 unless sufficient evidence is adduced to overturn this assumption [s.25 (3)].

- A person found guilty of a s.25 offence, if aged 18 or over at the time of the offence, is liable:
  - Where the touching has involved *penetration* of B's anus or *vagina* with a part of A's body or anything else, penetration of B's mouth with A's penis, penetration of A's anus or vagina with a part of B's body or penetration of A's mouth

with B's penis, on conviction on indictment (i.e. triable in the case of an adult only in the Crown Court) to imprisonment for up to 14 years
* In any other case, on summary conviction to a maximum 6 months imprisonment, a fine not exceeding the statutory maximum or both and on conviction on indictment to a maximum prison term of 14 years [s.25(4) & (6)]

NB. For a person aged less than 18, the maximum punishments are 6 months' imprisonment and/or a fine not exceeding the statutory maximum and on conviction on indictment to 5 years' imprisonment [s.25(5)].

Inciting a Child Family Member to Engage in Sexual Activity [s.26]

■ A person (A) commits an offence if:
* S/he intentionally incites another person (B) to touch, or allow her/himself to be touched by, A
* The touching is *sexual*
* The relation of A to B falls within those relationships defined in s.27 as a 'family relationship' (see below)
* Person A knows or could reasonably be expected to know that her/his relation to B does fall with one defined in s.27 and
* Either B is under 18 and A does not reasonably believe that B is 18 or over, or B is under 13 [s.26(1)]

NB. Where it is proved that B was under 18, it will be assumed the defendant knew this, unless sufficient evidence is adduced to raise an issue as to whether s/he reasonably believed B was 18 or over [s.26(2)]. It will also be assumed the defendant knew that her/his relation to B fell within one of those defined by s.27 unless sufficient evidence is adduced to overturn this assumption [s.26(3)].

- A person found guilty of a s.26 offence, if aged 18 or over at the time of the offence, is liable:
  - Where the touching has involved penetration of B's anus or *vagina* with a part of A's body or anything else, penetration of B's mouth with A's penis, penetration of A's anus or vagina with a part of B's body or penetration of A's mouth with B's penis,, on conviction on indictment (i.e. triable in the case of an adult only in the Crown Court), to imprisonment for up to 14 years
  - In any other case, on summary conviction to a maximum 6 months imprisonment, a fine not exceeding the statutory maximum or both and on conviction on indictment to a maximum prison term of 14 years [s.26(4) & (6)]

NB. For a person aged less than 18, the maximum punishments are 6 months' imprisonment and/or a fine not exceeding the statutory maximum and on conviction on indictment(i.e. triable in the case of an adult only in the Crown Court) to 5 years' imprisonment [s.26(5].

Family Relationships [s.27]

■ For the purposes of sexual offences, 'family relationships' are either the actual ones specified immediately below or those which would be so if an individual had not been adopted [s.27 (1)].

■ The relation of A to B is a s.27 'family relationship' if:
  • One of them is the other's parent, grandparent, brother, sister, half brother, half sister, aunt or uncles or
  • Person A is or has been B's foster parent [s.27(2)]

■ The relation of A to B is a s.27 'family relationship' if:
  • They have live or have lived in the same household, or A is or has been regularly involved in caring for, training, supervising or being in sole charge of B and
  • One of them is or has been the other's step-parent or A and B are cousins, or one of them is or has been the other's step-brother or step-sister, or the parent or present or former foster parent of one of them is or has been the other's foster parent [s.27(3)]

■ The relation of A to B is a s.27 'family relationship' if:
  • A and B live in the same household and
  • A is regularly involved in caring for, training, supervising or being in sole charge of B [s.27(4)]

Marriage Exception [s.28]

■ Conduct by a person (A) which would otherwise be an offence against person (B) under s. 25 or s.26 is not an offence if B is 16 or over and A and B are lawfully married [s.23].

NB. The defendant must prove that A and B were lawfully married at the time of any given conduct

Sexual Relationships which Pre-Date a 'Family Relationship' [s.29]

■ Unless that relationship is itself unlawful, conduct by a person (A) which would otherwise be an offence against another person (B) under s. 25 or s.26, is not an offence if:
   • The relation of A to B is other then those defined in s.27(2) i.e. one is a parent, grandparent, brother, sister, half-brother or half-sister, aunt or uncle or A is or has been B's foster parent
   • The relationship would not fall with s.27(2) if s.67 Adoption and Children Act 2002 did not apply or
   • Immediately before the relation of A to B first became one falling within s.27, a sexual relationship existed between A and B [s.29(1)&(2)]

NB. In ss.25–26. proceedings, it is for the defendant to prove the s.27(1) matters cited above [s.27(3).

Offences Against Persons with a Mental Disorder Impeding Choice

Sexual Activity with a Person with a Mental Disorder Impeding Choice [s.30]

- A person (A) commits an offence if:
  - S/he intentionally *touches* another person (B)
  - The touching is *sexual*
  - B is unable to refuse because of or for a reason related to a *mental disorder* and
  - Person A knows or could reasonably be expected to know that B has a mental disorder and that because of it or for a reason related to it, B is likely to be unable to refuse [s.30(1)]

- Person B is unable to refuse if:
  - S/he lacks the capacity to choose whether to agree to the touching (because s/he lacks sufficient understanding of the nature or reasonably foreseeable consequences of what is being done, or for any other reason) or
  - S/he is unable to communicate such a choice to person A [s.30(2)]

- A person guilty of a s.30 offence is:
  - **If** the touching involved penetration of B's anus or *vagina* with a part of A's body or anything else, *penetration* of B's mouth with A's penis, penetration of A's anus or vagina with a *part of B's body*, or penetration of A's mouth with B's

penis, liable on conviction on indictment (i.e. triable in the case of an adult only in the Crown Court) to imprisonment for life

- In any other case, on summary conviction liable to imprisonment for a maximum of 6 months, a fine not exceeding the statutory maximum or both, and on conviction on indictment, to a maximum of 14 years imprisonment [s.30(3)&(4)]

Causing or Inciting a Person with a Mental Disorder Impeding Choice to Engage in Sexual Activity [s.31]

- A person (A) commits an offence if:
  - S/he intentionally causes or incites another person (B) to engage in an activity
  - The activity is *sexual*
  - B is unable to refuse because of or for a reason related to a *mental disorder* and
  - Person A knows or could reasonably be expected to know that B has a mental disorder and that because of it or for a reason related to it, B is likely to be unable to refuse [s.31(1)]

- Person B is unable to refuse if:
  - S/he lacks the capacity to choose whether to agree to engaging in the activity caused or incited (because s/he lacks sufficient understanding of the nature or reasonably foreseeable consequences of the activity, or for any other reason) or

- S/he is unable to communicate such a choice to person A [s.31(2)]

■ A person guilty of a s.31 offence is:
  - **If** the activity cause or incited involved *penetration* of B's anus or *vagina*, penetration of B's mouth with a person's penis, penetration of a person's anus or *vagina* with a *part of B's body* or by B with anything else, or penetration of a person's mouth with B's penis, liable on conviction on indictment (i.e. triable in the case of an adult only in the Crown Court) to imprisonment for life
  - In any other case, on summary conviction liable to imprisonment for a maximum of 6 months, a fine not exceeding the statutory maximum or both, and on conviction on indictment, to a maximum of 14 years imprisonment [s.31(3)&(4)]

Engaging in Sexual Activity in the Presence of a Person with a Mental Disorder Impeding Choice [s.32]

■ A person (A) commits an offence if:
  - S/he intentionally engages in an activity
  - The activity is *sexual*
  - For the purposes of obtaining sexual gratification, /she engages in it when another person (B) is present or in a place from which person A can be *observed* and knowing or believing that B is aware, or intending that B should be aware that s/he is engaging in it

- B is unable to refuse because of or for a reason related to a *mental disorder* and
- Person A knows or could reasonably be expected to know that B has a mental disorder and that because of it or for a reason related to it, B is likely to be unable to refuse [s.32(1)]

■ Person B is unable to refuse if:
  - S/he lacks the capacity to choose whether to agree to being present (because s/he lacks sufficient understanding of the nature of the activity, or for any other reason) or
  - S/he is unable to communicate such a choice to person A [s.32(2)]

■ A person guilty of a s.32 offence is:
  - **If** the touching involved *penetration* of B's anus or *vagina* with a *part of A's body* or anything else, penetration of B's mouth with A's penis, penetration of A's anus or vagina with a part of B's body, or penetration of A's mouth with B's penis, liable on conviction on indictment (i.e. triable in the case of an adult only in the Crown Court) to imprisonment for life
  - In any other case, on summary conviction liable to imprisonment for a maximum of 6 months, a fine not exceeding the statutory maximum or both, and on conviction on indictment, to a maximum of 10 years imprisonment [s.32(3)&(4)]

Causing a Person, with a Mental Disorder Impeding Choice to Watch a Sexual Act [s.33]

- A person (A) commits an offence if:
  - For the purposes of obtaining sexual gratification, s/he intentionally causes another person (B) to watch a third person engaging in an activity, or to look at an *image* of any person engaging in an activity
  - The activity is *sexual*
  - B is unable to refuse because of or for a reason related to a *mental disorder* and
  - Person A knows or could reasonably be expected to know B has a mental disorder and because of it or for a reason related to it, B is likely to be unable to refuse [s.33(1)]

- Person B is unable to refuse if s/he:
  - Lacks the capacity to choose whether to agree to watching or looking (because s/he lacks sufficient understanding of nature of the activity, or any other reason) or
  - Is unable to communicate such a choice to person A [s.33(2)]

- A person guilty of a s.33 offence is:
  - On summary conviction liable to imprisonment for a maximum of 6 months, a fine not exceeding the statutory maximum or both
  - On conviction on indictment (i.e. triable in the case of an adult only in the Crown Court), to a maximum of 10 years imprisonment [s.33(3)]

Inducements etc to Persons with a Mental Disorder

Inducement, Threat or Deception to Procure Sexual Activity with a Person with a Mental Disorder [s.34]

- A person (A) commits an offence if:
  - With the agreement of another person (B), s/he intentionally *touches* that person
  - The touching is *sexual*
  - Person A obtains B's agreement by means of an inducement offered or given, a threat made or a deception practiced by A for that purpose
  - B has a *mental disorder* and
  - Person A knows or could reasonably be expected to know that B has a mental disorder [s.34(1)]

- A person guilty of a s.34 offence is:
  - **If** the touching involved *penetration* of B's anus or *vagina* with a *part of A's body* or anything else, penetration of B's mouth with A's penis, penetration of A's anus or vagina with a part of B's body, or penetration of A's mouth with B's penis, liable on conviction on indictment (i.e. triable in the case of an adult only in the Crown Court) to imprisonment for life
  - In any other case, on summary conviction liable to imprisonment for a maximum of 6 months, a fine not exceeding the statutory maximum or

both, and on conviction on indictment, to a
maximum of 14 years imprisonment
[s.34(2)&(3)]

Causing a Person with a Mental Disorder to Engage in or Agree to Engage in Sexual Activity by Inducement, Threat or Deception [s.35]

■ A person (A) commits an offence if:
  • By means of an inducement offered or given, a
    threat made or a deception practiced by
    her/him for this purpose, s/he intentionally
    causes another person (B) to engage in or agree
    to engage in, an activity,
  • The activity is *sexual*
  • B has a *mental disorder*
  • B is unable to refuse because of or for a reason
    related to a *mental disorder* and
  • Person A knows or could reasonably be expected
    to know that B has a mental disorder [s.35(1)]

■ A person guilty of a s.35 offence is:
  • **If** the activity caused or agreed to involved
    penetration of B's anus or *vagina*, penetration of
    B's mouth with a person's penis, penetration of a
    person's anus or vagina with a *part of B's body*
    or by B with anything else, or penetration of a
    person's mouth with B's penis, liable on
    conviction on indictment (i.e. triable in the case
    of an adult only in the Crown Court) to
    imprisonment for life
  • In any other case, on summary conviction liable

to imprisonment for a maximum of 6 months, a fine not exceeding the statutory maximum or both, and on conviction on indictment, to a maximum of 14 years imprisonment [s.35(2)&(3)]

Engaging in Sexual Activity in the Presence, Procurement by Inducement, Threat or Deception of a Person with a Mental Disorder [s.36]

■ A person (A) commits an offence if:
  - S/he intentionally engages in an activity
  - The activity is *sexual*
  - For the purpose of obtaining sexual gratification, s/he engages in it when another person (B) is present or is in a place from which A can be *observed*, and knowing or believing that B is aware, or intending that B should be aware, that s/he is engaging in it
  - B agrees to be present or in the place referred to in the place above because of an inducement offered or given, a threat made or a deception practiced by A for the purpose of obtaining that agreement
  - B has a *mental disorder* and
  - Person A knows or could reasonably be expected to know that B has a mental disorder [s.36(1)]

■ A person guilty of a s.36 offence is liable:
  - On summary conviction, to a maximum 6 months imprisonment, a fine not exceeding the statutory maximum or both

- On conviction on indictment (i.e. triable in the case of an adult only in the Crown Court), to imprisonment for a maximum of 10 years [s.36(2)]

Causing a Person with a Mental Disorder to Watch a Sexual Act by Inducement, Threat or Deception [s.37]

- A person (A) commits an offence if:
  - For the purposes of obtaining sexual gratification, s/he intentionally causes another person (B) to watch a third person engaging in an activity, or to look at an *image* of any person engaging in an activity
  - The activity is *sexual*
  - B agrees to watch or look because of an inducement offered or given, a threat made or a deception practiced by person A for the purpose of obtaining that agreement
  - B has a *mental disorder* and
  - Person A knows or could reasonably be expected to know that B has a mental disorder [s.37(1)]

- A person guilty of a s.37 offence is:
  - On summary conviction liable to imprisonment for a maximum of 6 months, a fine not exceeding the statutory maximum or both
  - On conviction on indictment (i.e. triable in the case of an adult only in the Crown Court), to a maximum of 10 years imprisonment [s.37(2)]

Care Workers for Persons with a Mental Disorder

Care Worker: Sexual Activity with a Person with a Mental Disorder [s.38]

■ A person (A) commits an offence if:
  - S/he intentionally *touches* another person (B)
  - The touching is *sexual* and
  - B has a *mental disorder*
  - A knows or could reasonably be expected to know that B has a mental disorder and
  - Person A is involved in B's care in a way described in s.42 summarised below [s.38(1)]

NB. Where in proceedings for s.38 offence it is proved the other person had a mental disorder, it will be assumed the defendant knew this, unless sufficient evidence is adduced to raise an issue as to whether s/he knew or could reasonably have been expected to know it[s.38(2)].

■ A person guilty of a s.38 offence is liable, on conviction on indictment (i.e. triable in the case of an adult only in the Crown Court) to a maximum 14 years imprisonment if the touching involved:
  - Penetration of B's mouth with A's penis
  - Penetration of A's anus or *vagina* with a *part of B's body* or
  - Penetration of a A's mouth with B's penis [s.38(3)]

- Unless the conditions above apply a person guilty of a s.38 offence is liable:
  - On summary conviction, to imprisonment for a maximum of 6 months, a fine not exceeding the maximum amount or both
  - On conviction on indictment, to a maximum of 10 years imprisonment [s.38(4)]

Care Workers: Causing or Inciting Sexual Activity [s.39]

- A person (A) commits an offence if:
  - S/he intentionally causes or incites another person (B) to engage in an activity
  - The activity is *sexual* and
  - B has a *mental disorder*
  - A knows or could reasonably be expected to know that B has a mental disorder and
  - Person A is involved in B's care in a way described in s.42 summarised below [s.39(1)]

  NB. Where in proceedings for s.39 offence it is proved the other person had a mental disorder, it will be assumed the defendant knew this, unless sufficient evidence is adduced to raise an issue as to whether s/he knew or could reasonably have been expected to know it [s.39(2)].

- A person guilty of a s.39 offence is liable, on conviction on indictment to a maximum 14 years imprisonment if the touching involved:
  - Penetration of B's anus or *vagina*
  - Penetration of B's mouth with a person's penis

- • Penetration of a person's anus or vagina with a part of B's body or by B with anything else
- • Penetration of a person's mouth with B's penis [s.39(3)]

■ Unless the conditions above apply, a person guilty of a s.39 offence is liable:
  - • On summary conviction, to imprisonment for a maximum of 6 months, a fine not exceeding the maximum amount or both
  - • On conviction on indictment (i.e. triable in the case of an adult only in the Crown Court), to a maximum of 10 years imprisonment [s.39(4)]

Care Workers: Sexual Activity in the Presence of a Person with a Mental Disorder [s.40]

■ A person (A) commits an offence if:
  - • S/he intentionally engages in an activity
  - • The activity is *sexual*
  - • For the purpose of obtaining sexual gratification, s/he engages in it when another person (B) is present or is in a place from which A can be *observed*, and knowing or believing that B is aware, or intending that B should be aware, that s/he is engaging in it
  - • B has a *mental disorder*
  - • A knows or could reasonably be expected to know that B has a mental disorder and
  - • Person A is involved in B's care in a way described in s.42 summarised below [s.40(1)]

NB. Where in proceedings for s.40 offence it is proved that the other person had a mental disorder, it will be assumed the defendant knew this, unless sufficient evidence is adduced to raise an issue as to whether s/he knew or could reasonably have been expected to know it[s.40(2)].

■ A person guilty of a s.40 offence is liable:
  • On summary conviction, to imprisonment for a maximum of 6 months, a fine not exceeding the maximum amount or both
  • On conviction on indictment (i.e. triable in the case of an adult only in the Crown Court), to a maximum of 7 years imprisonment [s.40(3)]

Care Workers: Causing a Person with a Mental Disorder to Watch a Sexual Act [s.41]

■ A person (A) commits an offence of causing a person with a mental disorder to watch a sexual act if:
  • For the purposes of obtaining sexual gratification, s/he intentionally causes another person (B) to watch a third person engaging in an activity, or to look at an *image* of any person engaging in an activity
  • The activity is *sexual*
  • B has a *mental disorder* and
  • Person A knows or could reasonably be expected to know that B has a mental disorder
  • Person A knows or could be reasonably be expected to know that B has a mental disorder and

- A is involved in B's care in a way that falls within s.42 summarised below [s.41(1)]

NB. Where in proceedings for s.41 offence it is proved the other person had a mental disorder, it will be assumed the defendant knew, unless sufficient evidence is adduced to raise an issue as to whether s/he knew or could reasonably have been expected to know [s.41(2)].

- A person guilty of a s.41 offence is:
  - On summary conviction liable to imprisonment for a maximum of 6 months, a fine not exceeding the statutory maximum or both
  - On conviction on indictment (i.e. triable in the case of an adult only in the Crown Court), to a maximum of 7 years imprisonment [s.41(2)]

Care Workers: Interpretation [s.42]

- For the purposes of ss.38–41 above, a person (A) is involved in the care of another person (B) if:
  - B is accommodated and cared for in a care home, community home, voluntary home or children's home and
  - Person A has functions to perform in the home in the course of employment which have brought her/him, or are likely to bring her/him into regular face to face contact with person B (including if B is a patient in NHS or independent medical agency /clinic / hospital or is a provider or care, assistance or services to

B in connection with her/his *mental disorder*
and as such likely to have regular face to face
contact with B [s.42(1)-(4)]

Marriage Exception [s.43]

■ Conduct by a person (A) which would otherwise be
an offence against person (B) under ss. 38–41 is not
an offence if B is 16 or over and A and B are lawfully
married [s.43].

*NB. The defendant must prove that A and B were
lawfully married at the time of any given conduct
[s.43 (2)].*

Sexual Relationships which Pre-Date 'Care Relationships' [s.44]

■ Unless that relationship is itself unlawful, conduct by
a person (A) which would otherwise be an offence
against another person (B) under ss.38–41 is not an
offence if:
  • Immediately before A became involved in B's
    care as defined in s.42, a sexual relationship
    existed between A and B [s.44(1)&(2)]

*NB. In ss.38–41 proceedings, it is for the defendant
to prove that such a relationship existed at that time
[s.44 (3)].*

Indecent Photographs of Children

- The Sexual Offences Act 2003 in ss.45–46 amends
  the provisions of the Protection of Children Act 1978
  and Criminal Justice Act 1988 with respect to
  indecent actual and pseudo-photographs.

Abuse of Children Through Prostitution & Pornography

Paying for Sexual Services of a Child [s.47]

- A person (A) commits an offence of paying for the sexual services of a child if:
  - S/he intentionally obtains for her/himself the sexual services of another person (B)
  - Before obtaining those services, s/he has made or promised payment for those services to B or a third person, or knows that another person has made or promised such a payment, and
  - Either B is under 18, and A does not reasonably believe that B is 18 or over, or B is under 13 [s.47(1)]

  NB. 'Payment' means any financial advantage, including the discharge of an obligation to pay or the provision of goods or services (including sexual services) gratuitously or at a discount [s.47 (2)].

- With the exception indicated below, a person guilty of as.47 offence against a person of under 16 is liable :
  - On conviction on indictment, to imprisonment for a maximum of 14 years if the offence involved *penetration* of B's anus or *vagina* with a *part of A's body* or anything else, penetration of B's mouth with A's penis, penetration of A's anus or vagina with a part of B's body or by B with anything else or penetration of A's mouth with B's penis

* In any other case, on summary conviction, to imprisonment for a maximum of 6 months, a fine not exceeding the statutory limit or both and on conviction on indictment (i.e. triable in the case of an adult only in the Crown Court) to a maximum of 14 years imprisonment [s.47(4)]

NB. A person guilty of an offence against a child aged under 13, is liable on conviction on indictment, to imprisonment for life, if the offence involved penetration of B's anus or vagina with a part of A's body or anything else, penetration of B's mouth with A's penis, penetration of A's anus or vagina with a part of B's body or by B with anything else or penetration of A's mouth with B's penis[s.47(3)].

Causing or Inciting Child Prostitution or Pornography [s.48]

■ A person (A) commits an offence of causing or inciting child prostitution or pornography if:
* S/he intentionally causes or incites another person (B) to become a prostitute, or to be involved in pornography, in any part of the world and
* Either B is under 18, and A does not reasonably believe that B is 18 or over or B is under 13 [s.48(1)]

■ A person guilty of a s.48 offence is liable:
* On summary conviction, to imprisonment for a maximum of 6 months, a fine not exceeding the statutory maximum or both

- On conviction on indictment (i.e. triable in the case of an adult only in the Crown Court), to imprisonment for a term not exceeding 14 years [s.48(2)]

Controlling a Child Prostitute or a Child Involved in Pornography [s.49]

■ A person (A) commits an offence of controlling a child prostitute or a child involved in pornography if:
  - S/he intentionally controls any activities of another person (B) relating to B's prostitution or involvement in pornography, in any part of the world and
  - Either B is under 18, and A does not reasonably believe that B is 18 or over, or B is under 13 [s.49(1)]

■ A person guilty of a s.49 offence is liable:
  - On summary conviction, to imprisonment for a maximum of 6 months, a fine not exceeding the statutory maximum or both
  - On conviction on indictment (i.e. triable in the case of an adult only in the Crown Court), to imprisonment for a term not exceeding 14 years [s.49(2)]

Arranging or Facilitating Child Prostitution or Pornography [s.50]

■ A person (A) commits an offence of arranging or facilitating child prostitution or pornography if:
  - S/he intentionally arranges or facilitates the

prostitution or involvement in pornography in
any part of the world of another person (B) and
* Either B is under 18, and A does not reasonably
believe that B is 18 or over, or B is under 13
[s.50(1)]

■ A person guilty of a s.50 offence is liable:
* On summary conviction, to imprisonment for a
maximum of 6 months, a fine not exceeding the
statutory maximum or both
* On conviction on indictment (i.e. triable in the
case of an adult only in the Crown Court), to
imprisonment for a term not exceeding 14 years
[s.50(2)]

*NB. For the purposes of ss.48–50, a person is
involved in pornography if an indecent image of
her/him is recorded. Prostitute means a person (A)
who, on at least 1 occasion and whether or not
compelled to do so, offers or provides sexual services
to another person in return for payment or a promise
of payment to A or to a third person [s.51 (1) & (2)].
Payment means any financial advantage, including
discharge of an obligation to pay or the provision of
goods and services (including sexual services)
gratuitously or at a discount [s.51 (3)].*

Exploitation of Prostitution

Causing or Inciting Prostitution for Gain [s.52]

- A person (A) commits an offence of causing or inciting prostitution for gain if:
  - S/he intentionally causes or incites another person to become a prostitute in any part of the world and
  - S/he does so for or in the expectation of gain for himself or a third person [s.52(1)]

- A person guilty of a s.52 offence is liable:
  - On summary conviction, to imprisonment for a maximum of 6 months, a fine not exceeding the statutory maximum or both
  - On conviction on indictment (i.e. triable in the case of an adult only in the Crown Court), to imprisonment for a term not exceeding 7 years [s.52(2)]

Controlling Prostitution for Gain [s.53]

- A person commits an offence of controlling prostitution for gain if s/he:
  - Intentionally controls any of the activities of another person relating to that person's prostitution in any part of the world and
  - Does so for, or in the expectation of gain for himself or a third person [s.53(1)]

- A person guilty of a s.53 offence is liable:
  - On summary conviction, to imprisonment for a

maximum of 6 months, a fine not exceeding the statutory maximum or both

- On conviction on indictment (i.e. triable in the case of an adult only in the Crown Court), to imprisonment for a term not exceeding 7 years [s.53(2)]

NB. In ss.52–53, gain means any financial advantage, including discharge of obligation to pay or provision of goods or services (including sexual) gratuitously or at a discount, or the good will of any person which is, or appears likely, in time , to bring financial advantage [s.55(1)]. Prostitute and prostitution are defined as in s.51 (2) above [s.54 (2)].

Amendments Relating to Prostitution

- The Sexual Offences Act 2003 in ss.55–56 and Sch.1 amend, with respect to prostitution, brothels etc the Sexual Offences Act 1956.

Trafficking

Trafficking into the UK for Sexual Exploitation [s.57]

■ A person commits an offence of trafficking into the UK for sexual exploitation if s/he intentionally arranges or facilitates the arrival in the United Kingdom of another person (B) and either s/he:
- Intends to do anything to or in respect of B, after B's arrival but in any part of the world, which if done will involved the commission of a relevant offence, or
- Believes that another person is likely to do something to or in respect of B, after B's arrival but in any part of the world, which if done will involve the commission of a relevant offence [s.57(1)]

■ A person guilty of a s.57 offence is liable:
- On summary conviction, to imprisonment for a maximum of 6 months, a fine not exceeding the statutory maximum or both
- On conviction on indictment (i.e. triable in the case of an adult only in the Crown Court), to imprisonment for a term not exceeding 14 years [s.57(2)]

Trafficking within the UK for Sexual Exploitation [s.58]

■ A person commits an offence of trafficking within the UK for sexual exploitation, if s/he intentionally arranges or facilitates travel within the United Kingdom of another person (B) and either s/he:
  • Intends to do anything to or in respect of B, during or after the journey and in any part of the world, which if done will involved the commission of a relevant offence, or
  • Believes that another person is likely to do something to or in respect of B, during or after the journey and in any part of the world, which if done will involve the commission of a relevant offence [s.58(1)]

■ A person guilty of a s.58 offence is liable:
  • On summary conviction, to imprisonment for a maximum of 6 months, a fine not exceeding the statutory maximum or both
  • On conviction on indictment (i.e. triable in the case of an adult only in the Crown Court), to imprisonment for a term not exceeding 14 years [s.58(2)]

Trafficking out of the UK for Sexual Exploitation [s.59]

■ A person commits an offence of trafficking out of the UK for sexual exploitation, if s/he intentionally arranges or facilitates the departure from the United Kingdom of another person (B) and either s/he:

- Intends to do anything to or in respect of B, after B's departure but and in any part of the world, which if done will involved the commission of a relevant offence, or
- Believes that another person is likely to do something to or in respect of B, after B's departure but in any part of the world, which if done will involve the commission of a relevant offence [s.59(1)]

- A person guilty of a s.59 offence is liable:
  - On summary conviction, to imprisonment for a maximum of 6 months, a fine not exceeding the statutory maximum or both
  - On conviction on indictment (i.e. triable in the case of an adult only in the Crown Court), to imprisonment for a term not exceeding 14 years [s.59(2)]

Preparatory Offences

Administering a Substance with Intent [s.61]

■ A person commits an offence of administering a substance with intent, if s/he intentionally administers a substance to, or causes a substance to be taken by, another person (B):
  • Knowing that B does not consent and
  • With the intention of stupefying or overpowering B, so as to enable any person to engage in a sexual activity that involves B [s.61(1)]

■ A person guilty of a s.61 offence is liable:
  • On summary conviction, to imprisonment for a maximum of 6 months, a fine not exceeding the maximum amount or both
  • On conviction on indictment(i.e. triable in the case of an adult only in the Crown Court), to a maximum of 10 years imprisonment [s.61(2)]

Committing an Offence with Intent to Commit a Sexual Offence [s.62]

■ A person commits an offence under s.62 if s/he commits any offence with the intention of committing a 'relevant sexual offence' i.e. any offence under Part 1 of this Act including aiding, abetting, counselling or procuring such an offence) [s.62(1) & (2)].

■ A person guilty of an offence under s.62 is liable on conviction on indictment, where the offence is committed by kidnapping or false imprisonment, to life imprisonment [s.62 (3)].

- In any other case, a person guilty of a s.62 offence is liable:
  - On summary conviction, to imprisonment for a maximum of 6 months, a fine not exceeding the statutory maximum or both
  - On conviction on indictment (i.e. triable in the case of an adult only in the Crown Court), to imprisonment for a term not exceeding 10 years [s.62(4)]

Trespass with Intent to Commit a Sexual Offence [s.63]

- A person commits an offence of trespass with intent to commit a sexual offence if s/he:
  - Is a trespasser on any premises
  - Intends to commit a relevant sexual offence on the premises
  - Knows that, or is reckless as to whether, s/he is a trespasser [s.63(1)]

  NB. Premises includes a structure or part of a structure; relevant sexual offence has he same meaning as in s.62 above and structure includes a tent, vehicle or other temporary or movable structure [s.63 (2)].

- A person guilty of a s.63 offence is liable:
  - On summary conviction, to imprisonment for a maximum of 6 months, a fine not exceeding the statutory maximum or both

- On conviction on indictment (i.e. triable in the case of an adult only in the Crown Court), to imprisonment for a term not exceeding 10 years [s.63(3)]

Sex with an Adult Relative

Sex with an Adult Relative: Penetration [s.64]

■ A person aged 16 or over (A) commits an offence of sex with an adult relative: penetration, if:
- S/he intentionally penetrates another person's *vagina* or anus with a *part of her/his body* or anything else, or penetrates another person's mouth with his penis
- The penetration is *sexual*
- The other person (B) is aged 18 or over
- A is related to B as defined below and
- A knows or could reasonably be expected to know that he is related to B in that way [s.64(1)]

■ The ways that A may be related to B are as parent, grandparent, child, grandchild, brother, sister, half-brother, half-sister, uncle, aunt, nephew or niece [s.64 (2)].

■ Where, in proceedings for a s.64 offence, it is proved that the defendant was related to the other person in any of the above ways, it is to be taken that the defendant knew or could reasonably have been expected to know that he was related in that way unless sufficient evidence is adduced to raise an issue as to whether s/he knew or could reasonably have been expected to know that s/he was [s.64 (4)].

■ A person guilty of a s.64 offence is liable:
- On summary conviction, to imprisonment for a

maximum of 6 months, a fine not exceeding the statutory maximum or both
- On conviction on indictment (i.e. triable in the case of an adult only in the Crown Court), to imprisonment for a term not exceeding 2 years [s.64(5)]

Sex with an Adult Relative: Consenting to Penetration [s.65]

- A person aged 16 or over (A) commits an offence of sex with an adult relative: consenting to penetration, if:
  - Another person (B) *penetrates* A's *vagina* or anus with a *part of B's body* or anything else, or penetrates A's mouth with B's penis
  - A consents to the penetration
  - The penetration is *sexual*
  - B is aged 18 or over
  - A is related to B in a way defined below and
  - A knows or could reasonably be expected to know that s/he is related to B in that way [s.65(1)]

- The ways that A may be related to B are as parent, grandparent, child, grandchild, brother, sister, half-brother, half-sister, uncle, aunt, nephew or niece [s.65 (2)].

- Where, in proceedings for a s.65 offence, it is proved that the defendant was related to the other person in any of the above ways, it is to be taken that the defendant knew or could reasonably have been expected to know that s/he was related in that way unless sufficient evidence is adduced to raise an issue as to whether s/he knew or could reasonably have been expected to know that s/he was [s.65 (4)].

■ A person guilty of a s.65 offence is liable:
  • On summary conviction, to imprisonment for a maximum of 6 months, a fine not exceeding the statutory maximum or both
  • On conviction on indictment (i.e. triable in the case of an adult only in the Crown Court) , to imprisonment for a term not exceeding 2 years [s.65(5)]

Other Offences

Exposure [s.66]

- A person commits an offence of exposure if s/he:
  - Exposes her/his genitals and
  - Intends that someone will see them and be caused alarm or distress [s.66(1)]

- A person guilty of a s.65 offence is liable:
  - On summary conviction, to imprisonment for a maximum of 6 months, a fine not exceeding the statutory maximum or both
  - On conviction on indictment (i.e. triable in the case of an adult only in the Crown Court), to imprisonment for a term not exceeding 2 years [s.66(2)]

Voyeurism [s.67]

- A person commits an offence of voyeurism, if:
  - For the purpose of obtaining sexual gratification, s/he *observes* another person doing a private act and
  - S/he knows that the other person does not consent to being observed for her/his sexual gratification [s.67(1)]

- A person commits an offence if s/he:
  - Operates equipment with the intention of enabling another person to observe, for the purpose of obtaining sexual gratification, a third person (B) doing a private act and

- Knows that B does not consent to her/him operating equipment with that intention [s.67(2)]

■ A person commits an offence if s/he:
  - Records another person (B) doing a private act
  - Does so with the intention that s/he or a third person will, for the purpose of obtaining sexual gratification, look at an *image* of B doing the act and
  - Knows that B does not consent to her/him recording the act with that intention [s.67(3)]

■ A person commits an offence if s/he installs equipment, or constructs or adapts a structure or part of a structure, with the intention of enabling her/himself or another person to commit an offence under s.67(1)

■ A person guilty of a s.67 offence is liable:
  - On summary conviction, to imprisonment for a maximum of 6 months, a fine not exceeding the statutory maximum or both
  - On conviction on indictment (i.e. triable in the case of an adult only in the Crown Court), to imprisonment for a term not exceeding 2 years [s.67(5)]

NB. For the purposes of s.67, a person is doing a private act if s/he is in a place which, in the circumstances, would reasonably be expected to provide privacy and the person's genitals, buttocks or breasts are exposed or covered only with underwear,

*s/he is using the lavatory or is doing a sexual act
that is not of a kind ordinarily done in public[s.68].
A 'structure' includes a tent, vehicle or vessel or other
temporary or movable structure [s.68(2)].*

Intercourse with an Animal [s.69]

- A person commits an offence of intercourse with an animal if:
  - He intentionally performs an act of *penetration* with his penis
  - What is penetrated is the *vagina* or *anus* of a living animal
  - He knows that, or is reckless as to whether, that is what is penetrated [s.69(1)]

- A person (A) commits an offence if:
  - A intentionally causes, or allows, A's vagina or anus to be penetrated
  - The penetration is by the penis of an animal and
  - A knows that, or is reckless as to whether, that is what A is being *penetrated* by [s.69(2)]

- A person guilty of a s.69 offence is liable:
  - On summary conviction, to imprisonment for a maximum of 6 months, a fine not exceeding the statutory maximum or both
  - On conviction on indictment (i.e. triable in the case of an adult only in the Crown Court), to imprisonment for a term not exceeding 2 years [s.69(3)]

Sexual Penetration of a Corpse [s.70]

- A person commits an offence of sexual penetration of a corpse if:
  - S/he intentionally performs an act of *penetration* with a part of her/his body or anything else
  - What is penetrated is a part of the body of a dead person
  - S/he knows that, or is reckless as to whether, that is what is penetrated and
  - The penetration is *sexual* [s.70(1)]

- A person guilty of a s.70 offence is liable:
  - On summary conviction, to imprisonment for a maximum of 6 months, a fine not exceeding the statutory maximum or both
  - On conviction on indictment (i.e. triable in the case of an adult only in the Crown Court), to imprisonment for a term not exceeding 2 years [s.70(1)]

Sexual Activity in a Public Lavatory [s.71]

- A person commits an offence of sexual activity in a public lavatory, if:
  - S/he is in a lavatory to which the public or a section of the public has or is permitted to have access, whether on payment or otherwise
  - S/he intentionally engages in an activity, and
  - The activity is sexual [s.71(1)]

> *NB. An activity is sexual if a reasonable person would, in all the circumstances but regardless of any person's purpose, consider it to be sexual [s.71(2)]*

- A person guilty of a s.71 offence is liable on summary conviction, to imprisonment for a maximum of 6 months, a fine not exceeding statutory maximum or both [s.71 (3)].

Offences outside the UK [s.72]

- With respect to offences specified in Sch. 2, an act done by a person in a country or territory outside the UK which constituted an offence under the law in force in that country or territory, and would constitute a sexual offence to which s.72 applies if it had been done in England, Wales or Northern Ireland constitutes that sexual offence under the law of that part of the UK [s.72 (1)].

> *NB. Proceedings under s.72 may only be brought against a person who was on 01.09.97, or has since become, a British citizen or resident in the UK [s.72 (2)].*

Supplementary and General

Exceptions to Aiding, Abetting & Counselling [s.73]

■ A person is not guilty of aiding, abetting or counselling the commission against a child of an offence to which s.73 applies if (as opposed to the purpose of obtaining sexual gratification or causing or encouraging the activity constituting the offence or the child's participation in it), s/he acts for the purpose of:
  - Protecting the child from sexually transmitted infection
  - Protecting the physical safety of the child
  - Preventing the child from becoming pregnant or
  - Promoting the child's emotional well-being by the giving of advice [s.73(1)]

■ S.73 offers protection to professionals acting in good faith and applies to offence under:
  - ss.5–7 (offences against children under 13)
  - s.9 (sexual activity with a child)
  - s.13 which would be an offence under s.9 if the offender were aged 18
  - Any of ss.16, 25, 30, 34 and 38 (sexual activity against a person aged under 16)

Part 2: Notifications & Orders

Notification Requirements

Persons Becoming Subject to Notification Requirements [s.80]

■ A person (for this purpose referred to as the 'relevant offender') is subject to the notification requirements of Part 2 for the period specified in s.82 and summarised in the table below if s/he is:
  • Convicted of an offence listed in Sch 3 of the Act
  • Found not guilty of such an offence by reason of insanity
  • Found to be under a disability and to have done the act charged against her/him in respect of such an offence
  • Cautioned (in England and Wales or Northern Ireland), in respect of such an offence [s.80(1)]

NB. Those persons who, at the time this Part comes into force, are subject to Part 1 Sexual Offenders Act 1997, will be subject to the notification requirements of this Act (unless her/his notification period has ended)[s.81]

S.81 contains further details of transitional arrangements for those formerly subject to the Sex Offenders Act 1997.

Notification Period for Relevant Offender

Description of Offender	*Notification Period*
Sentenced to life or 30 or more months imprisonment	Indefinite beginning with relevant date
Made subject of order under s.210F(1) Criminal Procedure (Scotland) Act 1995	Indefinite period beginning with that date
Admitted to hospital subject to a restriction order	Indefinite period beginning with that date
Sentenced to more than 6 & fewer than 30 months imprisonment	10 years beginning with that date
Sentenced to fewer than 6 months imprisonment	7 years beginning with that date
Admitted to hospital, not subject of a restriction order	7 years beginning with that date
A person within s.80(1)(d) i.e. cautioned	2 years beginning with that date
Conditional Discharge (in Scotland a Probation Order)	The period in that order
A person of any other description	5 years beginning with the relevant date

NB. Where a person is aged less than 18 on the relevant date, any determined notification period is halved [s.82 (2)].

■ For these purposes, 'relevant date' is defined by s.82(6) as being, in the case of a person within:
  • s.80(1)(a) or s.81(1)(a), the date of conviction
  • s.80(1)(b) or (c), or s.81(1)(b) or (c), the date of the finding
  • s.80(1)(d), the date of the caution
  • s.81(7), the date which, for the purposes of Part 1 Sex Offenders Act 1997, was the relevant date in relation to that person

Initial & Subsequent Notifications [ss.83 - 87]

■ A relevant offender must within 3 days notify the police of name, national insurance number, addresses etc as detailed in s.83 (5) [s.87(1)].

■ A relevant offender must also within 3 days notify the police of any change of name, address, stay at any address (7 days or 2 or more periods in a year totalling 7 days) not already notified to the police and other details as specified in s.84.

■ Unless the offender has provided information in accordance with s.84, s/he must provide annually the information required by s.83 [s.85].

- The Secretary of State may make regulations requiring relevant offenders who leave the UK to:
  - To notify the police of specified information (see below) and
  - If they subsequently return to the UK, to give other information to be specified in regulations [s.86(1)]

- A notification under s.86 must disclose:
  - The date on which the offender will leave the UK
  - The country (or first if more than one) to which s/he will travel and her/his point of arrival there
  - Any other information prescribed in the regulations which the offender holds about her/his departure from a and return to the UK

Young Offenders: Parental Directions [s.89]

- Where a young person aged less than 18 who is of the description in the first column of the following table, appears before the court referred to in column 2 alongside, the court may direct that s.89(2) (described immediately after the table) applies in respect of a parent with parental responsibility for that young offender [s.89(1)].

Description of Person	Court which may make the direction
Relevant offender within s.80(1)(a)–(c) or s.81(1)(a)–c) i.e. other than those who are cautioned	Court which deals with offender in respect of offence or finding
Relevant offender within s.129(1)(a)-(c) i.e. those breaching a RSHO or interim RHSO other than those cautioned	Court which deals with offender in respect of offence or finding
Person made subject of a final or interim notification order or final or interim sexual offences prevention order	Court which makes the order
Relevant offender defendant to application under s.89(4) or in Scotland s.89(5)	Court which hears the application

Parental Obligations

■ The obligations that would be imposed by or under ss.83–86 (initial, change and periodic notifications) are to be treated instead as obligations on the parent and s/he must ensure the young offender attends at the police station with her/him when a notification is being given [s.89(2)].

NB. A direction given under s.89(1) takes immediate effect and applies until the young person is 18 or such shorter period as the court may specify [s.89(3)].

Application by Police

■ A chief officer of police may by complaint to any
   magistrates court covering her/his area, apply for a
   s.89(1) direction with respect to a relevant offender:
   • Who is resident in her/his area, or who the chief
      officer believes is in, or intending to come to
      her/his police area
   • Who the chief officer believes is under 18
      [s.89(4)]

   *NB. This provision includes those offenders who
   receive a caution or final warning*

**Parental Directions: Variations, Renewals &
Discharges**

■ The following persons may (in England) apply to the
   appropriate court for an order varying, renewing or
   discharging a direction under s.89(1):
   • The young offender
   • Her/his parent
   • Chief officer of police for area in which young
      offender lives
   • A chief officer of police who believes the young
      offender is in, or is intending to come to her/his
      police area
   • Where the direction was made by an application
      under s.89(4), the chief officer who made it

Offences Relating to Notification [s.91]

- A person commits an offence if s/he:
  - Fails, without reasonable excuse, to comply with s.83 (1), 84 (1), 84(4)(b), 85(1), 87(4) or 89(2)(b), or any requirement imposed by regulations which may be made under s.86(1)
  - Notifies to the police information s/he know to be false in apparent compliance with the above notification requirements or with s.86(1) notifications about travel outside the UK [s.91(1)]

- A person guilty of a s.91 offence is liable:
  - On summary conviction, to imprisonment for a maximum of 6 months, a fine not exceeding the statutory maximum or both
  - On conviction on indictment (i.e. triable in the case of an adult only in the Crown Court), to imprisonment for a term not exceeding 5 years [s.91(2)]

Certificates for Purposes of Part 2 [s.92]

- If on any date a person is convicted of an offence listed in Sch.3, found not guilty of such an offence by reason of insanity or found to be under a disability and to have done the act with which s/he is charged and the court states this in open court and certifies it (at the time or subsequently):
  - The certificate is, for purposes of Part 2 evidence of those facts [s.92(1)&(2)]

- If the police (in England, Wales or Northern Ireland) caution an individual, inform her/him that the offence falls within Sch.3. and certify those facts (at the time or subsequently in such form as may be prescribed by the Secretary of State):
  - The certificate is, for purposes of Part 2 evidence of those facts [s.92(4)]

Information for Verification about Release or Transfer [ss.94–96]

■ Ss.94 and 95 provide the power to enable police to verify that an offender has notified the correct details in compliance with ss.83, 84 and 85 or with relevant sections of the Sex Offenders Act 1997.

■ S.96 re-enacts, with amendments, s.5B Sex Offenders Act 1997 and allows the Secretary of State to make regulations requiring those who are responsible for an offender whilst in detention to notify other relevant authorities of her/his release or transfer to another institution.

Notification Orders [ss.97–101]

Applications & Grounds [s.97]

- A chief officer of police may by complaint to any magistrates' court whose commission area includes any part of her/his police area, apply for a 'Notification Order' in respect of the defendant if:
  - It appears to her/him that the three conditions described below are met with respect to the defendant
  - The defendant resides in the police area or the chief officer believes that s/he is in, or intending to come to her/his police area

- The first condition is that under the law in force in a country outside of the UK:
  - S/he has been convicted of a 'relevant offence' (defined in s.99) and whether or not punished for it
  - A court exercising jurisdiction under that law has made in respect of a relevant offence, a finding equivalent to a finding that s/he is not guilty by reason of insanity
  - Such a court has made in respect of a relevant offence, a finding equivalent to a finding that s/he is under a disability and did he act of which s/he was accused
  - S/he has been cautioned in respect of a relevant offence [s.97(2)]

- The second condition is that:
  - The first condition is met because of a conviction, finding or caution which occurred on or after 01.09.97
  - The first condition is met because of a conviction or finding which occurred before that date, but the person was dealt with in respect of the offence or finding on or after that date, or has yet to be dealt with
  - The first condition is met because of a conviction or finding which occurred before that date, but on that date the person was, in respect of the offence or finding, subject under the law in force in the country concerned, to detention, supervision or any other disposal equivalent to any of those mentioned in s.81(3) read with s.81(6) and s.131 [s.97(3)]

- The third condition is that the notification period set out in s.82 has not expired [s.97 (4)].

Effect of Notification Order [s.98]

- Where an order is made, the offender will become subject to the notification requirements for the period set out in s.82 that applies to the sentence he received abroad.

- This period will run from the date of conviction or finding or caution abroad i.e. if a person was convicted abroad of an offence equivalent to the domestic offence of sexual assault and sentenced to

6 months' imprisonment, the notification period for the sentence of 6 months would be 7 years.

- ■ If the offender did not come to the UK until 5 years after the conviction, the notification requirements imposed under a Notification Order would only last for the remaining 2 of the 7 years since the date of conviction.

Relevant Offence [s.99]

- ■ In s.97 and s.98, 'relevant offence' means an act which:
  - • Constituted an offence under the law in the country concerned and
  - • Would have constituted an offence listed in Sch.3 (other than at paragraph 60 i.e. a specified type of offence in Scotland) if it had been done in any part of the UK [s.99(1)]

NB. The defendant may require the police to show that her/his offence, if committed in the UK would have constituted an offence listed in Sch.3. Otherwise, this is deemed to be accepted.

Interim Notification Order [s.100]

- ■ An application for an interim Notification Order may:
  - • Be made in the complaint containing the main application
  - • If the main application has been made, be made by the person who has made that application, by

> complaint to the court to which that application
> has been made [s.100(1)]

■ The court my, if it considers it just to do so, make an
interim Notification Order which will:
- Have effect only for a fixed period specified in
the order
- Cease to have effect, if it has not already done
so, on the determination of the main application
[s.100(3)&(4)]

■ The applicant or defendant may by complaint apply
to the court that made the interim Notification Order
for it to be varied, renewed or discharged [s.100 (7)].

Appeals [s.101]

■ A defendant may appeal to the Crown Court against
the making of an interim or full Notification Order.

Sexual Offences Prevention Order (SOPO)

■ The following material summarises the grounds and application processes for obtaining, and the effect of, a Sexual Offences Prevention Order (civil preventive orders intended to protect the public from serious sexual harm)

Application & Grounds [s.104]

■ A court may make a Sexual Offences Prevention Order where the conditions of s.104 (2) −(4) (see immediately below) are satisfied **and**:
   • In the case of subsection 4, it is satisfied that the defendant's behaviour since the appropriate date makes it necessary to make such an order, for the purposes of protecting the public or any particular members of the public from serious sexual harm from the defendant (s.104(1)(a)]
   • In any other case, it is satisfied that it is necessary to make such an order, for the purposes of protecting the public or any particular members of the public from serious sexual harm from the defendant [s.104(1)(b)]

■ The conditions of subsections 2 to 4 that must be satisfied if a s.104 order is to be made, are that **any** of the following applies to the defendant:
   • The court deals with her/him in respect of an offence listed in Sch.3 (sexual offences) or 5

(violent offences and those relating to trafficking, prostitution and child pornography) [s.104(2)]

- The court deals with her/him in respect of a finding that s/he is not guilty of a Sch.3 or 5 offence by reason of insanity or s/he is under a disability and has done the act charged against her/him in respect of such an offence [s.104(3)]
- An application under s.104(5) (see immediately below) has been made to the court in respect of her/him and on that application, it is proved s/he is a 'qualifying offender' as defined in s.106(6) or (7) summarised below [s.104(4)]

■ A chief officer of police may by complaint to a magistrates' court apply for an order in respect of a person who resides in her/his area or whom the chief officer believes is in, or intending to come to, her/his police area if it appears to her/him that the person:

- Is a 'qualifying offender' (defined immediately below) and
- Has, since the appropriate date acted in such a way as to give reasonable cause to believe that it is necessary for such an order to be made [s.104(5)]

NB. An application under s.104(5) may be made to any magistrates' court whose commission area includes any part of the applicant's police area or any place where it is alleged that the person acted in a way that gives reasonable cause to believe that such an order may be necessary [s.104(6)]

Qualifying Offender [s.106]

■ A person is a qualifying offender under s.106(6) if, whether before or after commencement of Part 2 of the Act, s/he has been:
  - Convicted of an offence listed in Sch.3 (other than at paragraph 60 i.e. a specified type of offence in Scotland) or in Sch.5
  - Found not guilty of such an offence by reason of insanity
  - Found to be under a disability and to have done the act charged against her/him in respect of such an offence or
  - In England and Wales or northern Ireland, cautioned in respect of such an offence

■ A person is a qualifying offender under s.106(7) if, whether before or after the commencement of Part 2 of the Act and under the law in force in a country outside the UK:
  - S/he has been convicted of a relevant offence (whether or not punished for it)
  - A court exercising jurisdiction under that law, has made in respect of a relevant offence, a finding equivalent to a finding that s/he is not guilty by reason of insanity
  - Such a court has made in respect of a relevant offence a finding equivalent to a finding that /she is under a disability and did the act charged against her/him in respect of the offence or
  - S/he has been cautioned in respect of a relevant offence

Effect of Sexual Offences Prevention Order [s.107]

- A Sexual Offences Prevention Order:
  - Prohibits the defendant from doing anything described in the order and
  - Has effect for affixed period (not less than 5 years) specified in the order or until further order [s.107(1)]

  NB. The only prohibitions that me be included in the order are those necessary for the purpose of protecting the public or any particular members of the public from serious sexual harm from the defendant [s.107(2)].

- The defendant remains subject to the notification requirements where:
  - An order is made in respect of a defendant who was a relevant offender immediately before the making of the order and
  - S/he would otherwise cease to be subject to the notification requirements of Part 2 whilst the order (as renewed from time to time) has effect [s.107(3)]

- Where an order is made in respect of a defendant who was not a relevant offender immediately before the making of the order:
  - The order causes the defendant to become subject to the notification requirements of Part 2 from the making of the order until the order (as renewed from time to time) ceases to have effect and

- Part 2 applies with the exception that the 'relevant date' is the date of the service of the order [s.107(4)&(5)]

Variations, Renewals and Discharges of Sexual Offences Prevention Order [s.108]

- The following persons may apply to the appropriate court for an order varying, renewing or discharging a Sexual Offences Prevention Order:
  - The defendant
  - The chief officer of police for the area in which the defendant resides
  - A chief officer of police who believes that the defendant is in, or is intending to come to, her/his police area
  - Where the order was made on the application under s.104(5), the chief officer of police who made it [s.108(1)&(2)]

- An application may be made where the 'appropriate court' is the Crown Court, in accordance with rules of court and in any other case, by complaint [s.108 (3)].

  NB. Where the Crown Court or Court of Appeal made the Sexual Offences Prevention Order, the Crown Court is the appropriate court. Where a magistrates court made the order, the appropriate court is that court, a magistrates' court for the area in which the defendant resides or, where the application is made by a chief officer of police, any magistrates' court whose commission area includes any part of the chief officer's police area.

*Where a youth court made the order, that court, a
youth court for the area in which the defendant
resides or, where the application is made by a chief
officer of police, any youth court whose commission
area includes any part of the chief officer's police
area is the appropriate court [s.108(7)].*

■ Subject to subsections 5 and 6 below, the court,
after hearing the person making the application and
(if they wish to be heard) the others mentioned in
subsection 2, may make any order, varying, renewing
or discharging the Sexual Offences Prevention Order,
that the court considers appropriate [s.108(4)].

■ An order may be renewed, or varied so as to impose
additional prohibitions on the defendant, only if it is
necessary to do so for the purposes of protecting the
public or any particular members of the public from
serious sexual harm from the defendant (and any
renewed or varied order may contain only such
prohibitions as are necessary for this purpose)
[s.108 (5)].

■ The court must not discharge an order before the end
of 5 years beginning with the day on which it was
made, without the consent of the defendant and:
  • Where the application is made by a chief officer
    of police, that chief officer or
  • In any other case, the chief officer of police for
    the area in which the defendant resides
    [s.108(6)]

Interim Sexual Offences Prevention Order [s.109]

■ Where an application under s.104(5) or s.105(1) (the main application) has not been determined, an application for an interim Sexual Offences Prevention Order:

- May be made by the complaint by which the main application is made, or
- If the main application has been made, may be made by the person who has made it, by complaint to the court to which that application has been made [s.109(2)]

■ The court may, if it considers it just make an interim Sexual Offences Prevention Order, prohibiting the defendant from doing anything described in the order [s.109(3)].

■ An interim order has effect only for a fixed period specified in the order and ceases to have effect, if it has not already done so, on determination of main application [s.109(4)].

NB. The effect of subsection 5 is to continue any pre-existing notification requirements for the duration of the Order if they would otherwise lapse, and to impose a notification requirement where none would otherwise was in force.

■ The applicant or the defendant may by complaint apply to the court that made the interim order for it to be varied, renewed or discharged [s.109 (6)].

Appeals Against interim or full Sexual Offences Prevention Order [s.110]

- A defendant may appeal against the making of a Sexual Offences Prevention Order, where:
    - S.104(2) applied (a Sch.3 or Sch.5 offence) as if the order were a sentence passed for that offence [s.110(1)(a)]
    - S. 104(3) (insanity / disability provisions) as if s/he had been convicted of the offence and the order were a sentence passed on her/him for that offence [s.110(1)(b)]
    - The order was made on an application under s.104(5), to the Crown Court [s.110(1)(c)]

- A defendant may appeal to the Crown Court against the making of an interim Sexual Offences Prevention Order [s.110 (2)].

- A defendant may appeal against the making of an order under s.108 (variations, renewals and discharges of SOPOs) or the refusal to make such an order:
    - Where the application for such an order was made to the Crown Court, to the Court of Appeal
    - In any other case, to the Crown Court [s.110(3)]

NB. An order made by the Crown Court on appeal, is to be treated as if it were made by the magistrates' court that imposed the original order, for the purposes of determining where any application for variation, renewal or discharge should be heard under ss.108 or 109 [s.110(5)].

S.110 (1)(a) and (b) equate the making of a SOPO to a sentence in criminal proceedings, therefore s.100 Magistrates' Courts Act 1980 applies to the effect that the decision of he Crown Court has effect as if it had been made by magistrates' court against whose decision the appeal is being brought. Accordingly, s.100 of the Sexual Offences Act 2003 sub-sections 1(1),(2),93) make equivalent provisions for circumstances not covered by s.110 Magistrates' Courts Act 1980.

Breach of interim or full Sexual Offences Prevention Order [s.113]

■ A person commits an offence if, without reasonable excuse, s/he does anything which s/he is prohibited from doing by:
  • A Sexual Offences Prevention Order
  • An interim Sexual Offences Prevention Order
  • An order under s.5A Sex Offenders Act 1997 (Restraining Order)
  • An order under ss.2, 2A or 20 Crime and Disorder Act 1998 (Sex Offender Orders and interim orders made in England and Wales and Scotland)
  • An order under Article 6 or 6A Criminal Justice (Northern Ireland) Order 1998 (Sex Offender Orders and interim orders made in Northern Ireland) [s.113(1)]

■ A person guilty of an offence under s.113 is liable:
  • On summary conviction, to imprisonment for a

term not exceeding 6 months, a fine not
exceeding the statutory maximum or both

- On conviction on indictment, to imprisonment
for a term not exceeding 5 years [s.113(2)]

*NB. The court cannot grant a Conditional Discharge
to a person convicted under s.113 [s.113(3)].*

Foreign Travel Order (FTO)

■ A Foreign Travel Order is a new civil preventive order and enables the courts to prohibit certain persons from travelling abroad where it is necessary to protect a child from serious sexual harm outside the UK.

Applications & Grounds for Foreign Travel Order [s.114]

■ A chief officer of police may by complaint to a magistrates' court apply for a Foreign Travel Order in respect of a person who resides in her/his police area or who the chief police officer believes is in, or is intending to come to her/his police area, if it appears to the chief officer that the defendant:
  • Is a 'qualifying offender' and
  • Has since the appropriate date, acted in such a way as to give reasonable cause to believe that is necessary for such an order to be made [s.114(1)]

NB. An application may be made to any magistrates' court whose commission area includes any part of the applicant's police area [s.114 (2)].

■ On the application, the court may make a Foreign Travel Order if it is satisfied that:
  • The defendant is a qualifying offender and
  • The defendant's behaviour since the appropriate date makes it necessary to make such an order, for the purposes of protecting children generally

or any child from serious sexual harm from the defendant outside the UK [s.114(3)]

NB. In s.114, protecting children means protecting persons aged under 16 (17 in Northern Ireland) generally or any particular person aged under 16 (17 in Northern Ireland) from serious physical or psychological harm caused by the defendant doing, outside the UK, anything which would constitute an offence listed in Sch.3 if done in any part of the UK [s.115]

- A person is a 'qualifying offender' for the purposes of s.114 if, whether before or after commencement of Part 2 s/he has been:
  - Convicted of an offence within subsection 2 below
  - Found not guilty of such an offence by reason of insanity
  - Found to be under a disability and to have done the act charged against her/him in respect of such an offence or
  - In England, Wales or Northern Ireland, cautioned in respect of such an offence [s.116(1)]

- The offences referred to in subsection 2 are:
  - An offence within any of the paragraphs 13 to 15, 44 to 46, 77, 78 and 82 of Sch.3
  - An offence within paragraph 31 of that Schedule, if the intended offence was an offence against a person aged under 16
  - An offence within paragraph 93 of that Schedule if the corresponding civil offence is an

offence within any of paras. 13 to 15 of that Schedule, or the corresponding civil offence is an offence within paragraph 31 and the intended offence was against a person aged under 16, or the corresponding civil offence is an offence within any of paras.1 to 12, 16 to 30 and 32 to 35 and the victim of the offence was under 16 at the time of the offence [s.116(2)]

- A person is also a qualifying offender for the purposes of s.114 if, under the law in force in a country outside he UK and whether before or after the commencement of Part 2:
  - S/he has been convicted of a 'relevant offence' (whether or not s/he has been punished for it)
  - A court exercising jurisdiction under that law has made in respect of a relevant offence a finding equivalent to a finding that s/he is not guilty by reason of insanity
  - Such a court has made in respect of a relevant offence a finding equivalent to a finding that s/he is under a disability and did the act charged against her/him in respect of the offence [s.116(3)]
  - S/he has been cautioned in respect of a relevant offence

NB. In s.116(3) relevant offence means an act which constituted an offence under the law in force in the country concerned and would have constituted an offence within subsection 2 if it had been done in any part of the UK [s.116(4)].

NB. The defendant may require the police to show that her/his offence, if committed in the UK would have constituted an offence within subsection 2.

Effect of Foreign Travel Order [s.117]

- A Foreign Travel Order has effect for a fixed period of not more than 6 months specified in the order [s.117 (1].

- The order prohibits the defendant from doing whichever of the following is specified in the order:
  - Travelling to any country outside the UK named or described in the order
  - Travelling to any country outside the UK other than a country named or described in the order
  - Travelling to any country outside the UK [s.117(2)]

- The only prohibitions that may be included in the order are those necessary for the purpose of protecting children generally or any child from serious sexual harm from the defendant outside the UK [s.117(3)] and for the purposes of s.117, 'protecting children generally etc' has the same definition as in s.115 (2) provided above.

- If at any time while an order (as renewed from time to time) has effect a defendant is not a relevant offender, the order causes him to be subject to the requirements imposed by regulations made under s.86(1) (and for these purposes, the defendant is to be treated as if s/he were a relevant offender). [s.117 (4)].

NB. Where a court makes a Foreign Travel Order in relation to a person already subject to such an order (whether made by that court or another), the earlier order ceases to have effect [s.117(5)].

Variations, Renewals & Discharges of Foreign Travel Order [s.118]

■ The following persons may by complaint to the appropriate court apply for an order varying, renewing or discharging a Foreign Travel Order:
  • The defendant
  • The chief officer of police on whose application the Foreign Travel Order was made
  • The chief officer of police for the area in which the defendant resides
  • A chief officer of police who believes that the defendant is in, or is intending to come to, her/his police area [s.118(1)&(2)]

■ The court, after hearing the person making the application and (if they wish to be heard) the other persons cited in subsection 2, may make any order, varying, renewing or discharging a Foreign Travel Order [s.118(3)]

NB. An order may be renewed or varied so as to impose additional prohibitions on the defendant, only if it is necessary to do so for the purpose of protecting children generally, or any child from serious harm from the defendant outside he UK (and any renewed or varied order may contain only such prohibitions as are necessary for this purpose [s.118(4)]

For the purposes of s.118, the appropriate court means the court which made the Foreign Travel Order, a magistrates' court for the area in which the defendant lives or, where the application is made by a chief officer of police, any magistrates' court whose commission area includes any part of her/his police area [s.118(5)].

Appeals against Foreign Travel Order [s.119]

- A defendant may appeal to the Crown Court:
  - Against the making of a Foreign Travel Order
  - Against the making of an order under s.118 or the refusal to make such an order

- On any such appeal, the Crown Court may make such orders as may be necessary to give effect to its determination of the appeal, and may also make such incidental or consequential orders as appear to it to be just [s.119(2)].

NB. Any order made by the Crown Court on an appeal under subsection (1)(a) (the making of a Foreign Travel Order), other than an order directing that an application be re-heard by a magistrates' court, is for the purposes of s.118 (5) (determination of 'appropriate court'), to be treated as if it were an order of the court from which the appeal was brought, not an order of the Crown Court [s.119 (3)].

Breach of Foreign Travel Order [s.122]

■ A person commits an offence if, without reasonable excuse, s/he does anything which he is prohibited from doing by a Foreign Travel Order [s.122 (1)].

■ A person guilty of an offence under s.122 is liable:
  • On summary conviction, to imprisonment for a term not exceeding 6 months, a fine not exceeding the statutory limit or both
  • On conviction on indictment, to imprisonment for a term not exceeding 5 years [s.122(2)]

  NB. The court cannot grant a Conditional Discharge to a person convicted under s.122 [s.122 (3)].

Risk of Sexual Harm Order

Applications, Grounds & Effect of Risk of Sexual Harm Order [s.122]

- A chief officer of police may by complaint to a magistrates' court apply for a Risk of Sexual Harm Order in respect of a person aged 18 or over who resides in her/his police area or who the chief police officer believes is in, or is intending to come to her/his police area, if it appears to the chief officer that:
  - The defendant has on at least 2 occasions, whether before or after commencement of Part 2 of this Act, done an act which falls within subsection 3 (described below) [s.123(1)(a)] and
  - As a result of those acts, there is reasonable cause to believe that it is necessary for such an order to be made [s.123(1)(b)]

- An application may be made to any magistrates' court whose commission area includes:
  - Any part of the applicant's police area
  - Any place where it is alleged that the defendant acted in a way mentioned in subsection (1)(a) (described below)

- The acts are:
  - Engaging in sexual activity involving a child or in the presence of a child
  - Causing or inciting a child to watch a person engaging on sexual activity or to look at a moving or still image that is sexual

- • Giving a child anything that relates to sexual
    activity or contains a reference to such activity
- • Communicating with a child, where any part of
    the communication is sexual [s.123(3)]

■ On the application, the court may make a Risk of
Sexual Harm Order if it is satisfied that:
- • The defendant has on at least 2 occasions,
    whether before or after commencement of s.123,
    done an act falling within subsection (3) and
- • It is necessary to make such an order, for the
    purposes of protecting children generally or any
    child from harm from the defendant [s.123(4)]

■ Such an order:
- • Prohibits the defendant from doing anything
    described in he order
- • Has effect for a fixed period (not less than 2
    years) specified in the order or until further order
    [s.123(5)]

■ The only prohibitions that may be imposed are those
necessary for the purpose of protecting children
generally or any child from harm from the defendant
[s.123 (6)].

*NB. Where a court makes a Risk of Sexual Harm
Order in relation to a person already subject to such
an order (made by that court or another), the earlier
order ceases to have effect [s.123(7)].*

- **For the purpose of s.123** the following definitions apply:
  - **Protecting children generally or any child from harm from the defendant** means protecting children generally or any child from physical or psychological harm, caused by the defendant doing acts that fall within s.123(3)
  - **Child** means a person under 16 (or 17 in Northern Ireland)
  - **Image** means an image produced by any means, whether of a real or imaginary subject
  - **Sexual activity** means an activity that a reasonable person would, in all the circumstances but regardless of any person's purpose, regard to be sexual
  - **Sexual communication** means communication in which any part of it relates to sexual activity or a reasonable person would, in all the circumstances, but regardless of any person's purpose, consider any part of it to be sexual
  - **Sexual Image** means an image of which any part relates to sexual activity or a where a reasonable person would, in all the circumstances, but regardless of any person's purpose, consider any part of it to be sexual [s.124]

Variations, Renewals & Discharges of Risk of Sexual Harm Order [s.125]

- The following persons may by complaint apply to the appropriate court for an order varying, renewing or discharging a Risk of Sexual Harm Order:
  - The defendant
  - The chief officer of police on whose application the Risk of Sexual Harm Order was made
  - The chief officer of police for the area in which the defendant resides
  - A chief officer of police who believes that the defendant is in, or is intending to come to, her/his police area

- Subject to subsections 4 and 5 below, the court, after hearing the person making the application and (if they wish to be heard) the others mentioned in subsection 2, may make any order, varying, renewing or discharging the Risk of Sexual Harm Order, that the court considers appropriate [s.125(3)]

- An order may be renewed, or varied so as to impose additional prohibitions on the defendant, only if it is necessary to do so for the purposes of protecting children generally or any child from harm from the defendant - defined in s.124 (2) above (and any renewed or varied order may contain only such prohibitions as are necessary for this purpose) [s.125 (4)].

- The court must not discharge an order before the end of 2 years beginning with the day on which it was made, without the consent of the defendant and:

- Where the application is made by a chief officer of police, that chief officer or
- In any other case, the chief officer of police for the area in which the defendant resides [s.125(5)]

NB. For the purposes of s.125, the appropriate court means the court which made the Risk of Sexual Harm Order, a magistrates' court for the area in which the defendant lives or, where the application is made by a chief officer of police, any magistrates' court whose commission area includes any part of her/his police area [s.125(7)].

Interim Risk of Sexual Harm Order [s.126]

- Where an application under s.125(1) (the main application) has not been determined, an application for an interim Sexual Offences Prevention Order:
  - May be made by the complaint by which the main application is made, or
  - If the main application has been made, may be made by the person who has made it, by complaint to the court to which that application has been made [s.126 (1) & (2)]

- The court may, if it considers it just to do so, make an interim Risk of Sexual Harm Order, prohibiting the defendant from doing anything described in the order [s.126(3)].

■ An interim order has effect only for a fixed period specified in the order and ceases to have effect, if it has not already done so, on determination of main application [s.126(4)].

■ The applicant or the defendant may by complaint apply to the court that made the interim order for it to be varied, renewed or discharged [s.126 (5)].

Appeals against interim or full Risk of Sexual Harm Order [s.127]

■ A defendant may appeal to the Crown Court against the making of a:
  • Risk of Sexual Harm Order
  • Interim Risk of Sexual Harm Order
  • An order under s.125 or the refusal to make such an order [s.127(1)]

■ On any such appeal, the Crown court may make such orders as may be necessary to give effect to its determination of the appeal, and may also make such incidental or consequential orders as appear to it to be just [s.127(2)]

NB. An order made by the Crown Court on an appeal under subsection (1)(a) or (b) – other than an order directing that an application be re-heard by a magistrates' court – is, for purposes of s.125(7) or s.126(5) respectively, to be treated as if it were an order of the court from which the appeal was brought not an order of the Crown Court [s.127(3)].

Breach of interim or full Risk of Sexual Harm Order [s.128]

■ A person commits an offence if, without reasonable excuse, s/he does anything which s/he is prohibited from doing by:
  • A Risk of Sexual Harm Order
  • An interim Risk of Sexual Harm Order

■ A person guilty of an offence under s.128 is liable:
  • On summary conviction, to imprisonment for a term not exceeding 6 months, a fine not exceeding the statutory maximum or both
  • On conviction on indictment, to imprisonment for a term not exceeding 5 years [s.128(2)]

NB. The court cannot grant a Conditional Discharge to a person convicted under s.128 [s.128 (3)].

Effect of Conviction etc under s.128 [s.129]

■ S. 129 applies to a person who is:
  • Convicted of an offence under s.128
  • Found not guilty of such an offence by reason of insanity
  • Found to be under a disability and to have done the act charged against her/him in respect of such an offence or
  • Cautioned in respect of such an offence

■ The defendant remains subject to notification requirements where s/he:
  • **Was a relevant offender** immediately before s.129 applied to her/him and

- Would (apart from this section) cease to be subject to notification requirements of Part 2 of the Act while the relevant order (as renewed from time to time) has effect [s.129(2)]

■ Where the defendant **was not a relevant offender** immediately before s.129 applied to her/him:
- This section causes the defendant to become subject to the notification requirements of Part 2 from the time the section first applies to her/him until the relevant order (as renewed from time to time) ceases to have effect and
- Part 2 applies to the defendant from the date on which this section applies to that defendant [s.129(3)]

Appendix 1: CAE Publications

- Personal Guides:
    - Children Act 1989 in the Context of the Human Rights Act 1998
    - Childminding and Day Care (England)
    - Child Protection
    - Residential Care of Children
    - Fostering
    - 'How Old Do I Have To Be...?' (simple guide to the rights and responsibilities of 0–21 year olds)
    - Domestic Violence – (Part IV Family Law Act 1996 & Protection from Harassment Act 1997)
    - Looking After Children: Good Parenting, Good Outcomes (DH LAC System)
    - Crime and Disorder Act 1998
    - Sexual Offences Act 2003
    - Anti Social Behaviour

All available from: 103 Mayfield Road, South Croydon, Surrey CR2 0BH tel: 020 8651 0554 fax: 020 8405 8483 email: childact@dial.pipex.com

www.caeuk.org

Discounts for orders of 50 or more of any one title